Understanding the Elements of the Periodic Table™

IRON

Heather Hasan

26   56

Fe

rosen
central™

The Rosen Publishing Group, Inc., New York

For Omar, my husband and best friend. It is an absolute joy to share my life with you.

Published in 2005 by The Rosen Publishing Group, Inc.
29 East 21st Street, New York, NY 10010

Library of Congress Cataloging-in-Publication Data

Hasan, Heather.
Iron / by Heather Hasan.
     p. cm.—(Understanding the elements of the periodic table)
Summary: Explains the characteristics of iron, where it is found, how it is used by humans, and its relationship to other elements found in the periodic table.
Includes bibliographical references and index.
ISBN 1-4042-0157-2 (library binding)
1. Iron—juvenile literature. [1. Iron. 2. Periodic law—Tables.] I. Title. II. Series.
QD181.F4H375 2004
669'.14—dc22
                                                    2003022262

On the cover: Iron's square on the periodic table of elements. Inset: The subatomic makeup of the iron atom.

Manufactured in the United States of America

Contents

Introduction

Have you ever wished upon a shooting star? That bright streak of light that you saw in the sky was actually a small piece of solid matter called a meteoroid, falling through Earth's atmosphere. Meteoroids contain iron (Fe), among other things. When meteoroids enter Earth's atmosphere, they are going very fast and get very hot. Most meteoroids burn up before crashing onto Earth's surface.

Sometimes, some of the meteoroid doesn't burn up, and it falls to Earth as a meteorite. Meteorites are made of a mixture, or alloy, of iron and nickel (Ni). Archaeologists searching the tombs of ancient Egyptians have found tools and beaded jewelry that were made with iron. Some of these items date back to 4000 BC! If the Egyptians had used pure iron found in Earth's crust, their tools would have long since rusted and crumbled away. However, the iron that the Egyptians used contained a tiny bit of another metal—nickel. So the Egyptians also noticed shooting stars, just as you have.

Because the Egyptians saw their source of iron falling from the sky, they called this metal *ba-ne-pe*, which means "metal of heaven." They believed that iron fell from the sky as a gift from the gods. This metal was rare and was prized by these ancient people.

Since that time, we have found other, more abundant sources of iron on Earth. Iron and its alloys are much more common today and

Iron has always been found in iron-nickel meteorites *(above)*. The iron found in meteorites is an alloy, or a mixture of metallic elements. Today, iron is mined from Earth's crust, where it is trapped with other minerals in iron ore.

can be found in things all around us. Iron, like every other element on the periodic table, acts as a building block. Iron lends itself to creating and sustaining many things throughout our universe. Iron is everywhere, from meteors hurling through outer space, to blood cells coursing through our bodies. This is the story of iron.

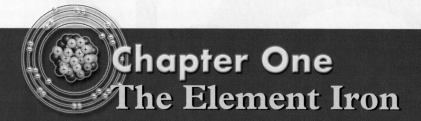

Chapter One
The Element Iron

You are probably quite familiar with the element iron. The word "iron" comes from the Anglo-Saxon language. Iron's chemical symbol, Fe, comes from the Latin word for iron, *ferrum*. Iron is the metal on which modern civilization is built. In its pure form, iron is used in tools, in washing machines, and in cars. Pure iron is a shiny silver-colored metal. Unfortunately, pure iron rusts very quickly when exposed to air and moisture. Iron is much more useful when it is combined with other substances in an alloy to make steel. These other substances can be nickel, carbon (C), chromium (Cr), and titanium (Ti). Steel is used to make many things, from paper clips to skyscrapers. Iron is one of the most important and abundant elements in our world.

Everything Is Made Up of Elements

Nearly everything in the universe is composed of one or more elements. An element is a substance that cannot be broken down into smaller parts by natural means. Each element is made up of only one kind of atom, and each atom of iron is exactly the same. Atoms are very tiny. It would take 200 million average-size atoms, lying side by side, to form a line that is only 0.4 inch (1 centimeter) long! Amazingly, atoms are made up of even smaller components—subatomic particles.

Subatomic Particles

There are three major subatomic particles that make up the atom: neutrons, protons, and electrons. Neutrons and protons are clustered together at the center of the atom to form a dense core called the nucleus. Neutrons carry no electric charge, while protons have a positive electrical charge. This gives the nucleus an overall positive electrical charge. Iron has twenty-six protons in its nucleus, so its nucleus has a charge of +26.

Around the nucleus of an atom are negatively charged electrons, arranged in layers around the nucleus called shells. The electrons are not fixed in a single position, but orbit, or circle, around the nucleus. Why do the electrons remain in orbit? The negative electrons are attracted to the positive nucleus, and it is this attraction that holds the electrons around the nucleus. So that the positive and negative charges of the atom balance, the number of protons and electrons are almost always equal. Therefore, since iron has twenty-six protons, it also has twenty-six electrons.

All atoms are made up of the subatomic particles protons, neutrons, and electrons. The iron atom is fairly complex. It contains twenty-six protons and thirty neutrons in its nucleus. Twenty-six electrons surround the nucleus.

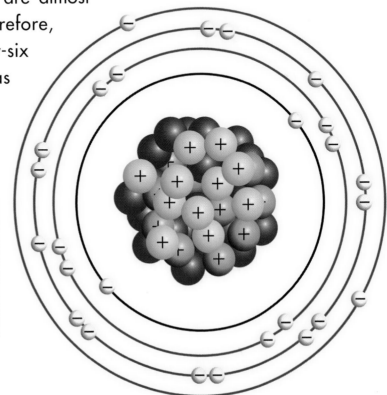

Iron Snapshot

Chemical Symbol:	Fe
Properties:	Transition metal; silver color; solid at room temperature
Discovered By:	Was known by ancient civilizations
Atomic Number:	26
Atomic Weight:	55.845
Protons:	26
Electrons:	26
Neutrons:	30
Density at 293 K:	7.86 g/cm^3 at 1 atm
Melting Point:	2,795°F; 1,535°C; 1,808 K
Boiling Point:	4,982°F; 2,750°C; 3,023 K
Commonly Found:	Earth's crust as iron ore; meteorites

The Periodic Table

Today there are more than 100 known elements. As more elements were discovered over the years, they had to be organized somehow. Scientists eventually arranged the elements on a big chart, called the periodic table of elements. The periodic table that we use today is based on the work of Russian chemist Dmitry Mendeleyev, who published the first version of the table in 1869 while teaching chemistry at the University of St. Petersburg in Russia. Mendeleyev sought to organize the elements in a

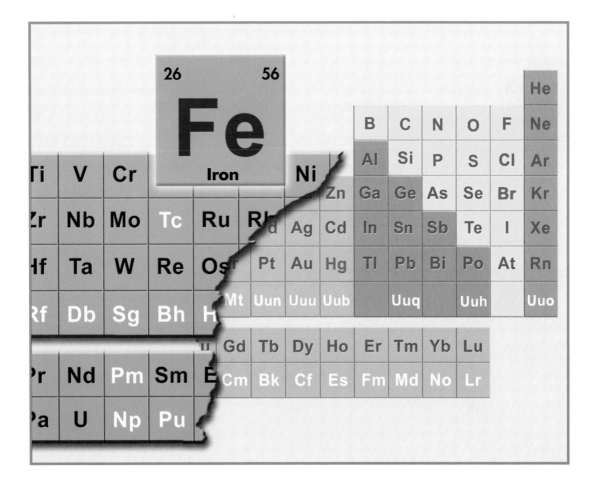

Russian scientist Dmitry Mendeleyev developed the periodic table in order to organize the elements. Iron occupies the twenty-sixth square on the periodic table. It is one of many metals, including nickel, silver (Ag), and cobalt (Co).

way that would make it easier for his students to study and understand them. He arranged the elements in horizontal rows according to atomic weight, with the lightest element of each row on the left and the heaviest on the right. Though Mendeleyev's periodic table did not list all of the elements that we know of today, iron was among those that he included.

Today, the elements on the periodic table are listed in order of increasing atomic number, which is the atom's number of protons. Arranged like this, many trends, or patterns, can be seen. You can use these trends to help you classify the elements. By seeing where an element is found on the periodic table, you can predict whether it is a metal, a nonmetal, or a metalloid. Metals can be recognized by their physical traits. Generally, metals can be polished to be made shiny. We also know that metals conduct electricity. Most metals also have the ability to be hammered into shapes without breaking. This is called malleability. Metals are also usually ductile, which means that they can be pulled into wires. Substances such as plastics, glass, and wood are classified as nonmetals, because they lack the characteristics of metals. Metalloids, or semimetals, have characteristics of both metals and nonmetals. In most respects, metalloids behave like nonmetals. However, they are able to conduct electricity, though not nearly as well as metals do.

The elements on the periodic table are divided by a "staircase" line. The metals are found to the left of this line and the nonmetals are on the right. Most of the elements bordering the staircase line are metalloids. Iron, as you would expect, is located to the left of the staircase line.

Groups and Periods

The periodic table is very useful because we can tell a lot about an element just by seeing where it is located on the table. As you look across the table from left to right, the horizontal line of elements is called a period. Elements

VIIIB	VIIIB	VIIIB	IB	IIB	IIIA	IVA	VA	VIA	VIIA
8	9	10	11	12	13	14	15	16	17

Group

Period

| | | | | | | 5 11 **B** Boron | 6 12 **C** Carbon | 7 14 **N** Nitrogen | 8 16 **O** Oxygen | 9 19 **F** Fluorine |

| | | | | | | 13 27 **Al** Aluminum | 14 28 **Si** Silicon | 15 31 **P** Phosphorus | 16 32 **S** Sulfur | 17 35 **Cl** Chlorine |

| Cr | Mn | 26 56 **Fe** Iron | 27 59 **Co** Cobalt | 28 59 **Ni** Nickel | 29 64 **Cu** Copper | 30 65 **Zn** Zinc | 31 70 **Ga** Gallium | 32 73 **Ge** Germanium | 33 75 **As** Arsenic | 34 79 **Se** Selenium | 35 80 **Br** Bromine |

| Mo | | 44 101 **Ru** Ruthenium | 45 103 **Rh** Rhodium | 46 106 **Pd** Palladium | 47 108 **Ag** Silver | 48 112 **Cd** Cadmium | 49 115 **In** Indium | 50 119 **Sn** Tin | 51 122 **Sb** Antimony | 52 128 **Te** Tellurium | 53 127 **I** Iodine |

| W | Re | 76 190 **Os** Osmium | 77 192 **Ir** Iridium | 78 195 **Pt** Platinum | 79 197 **Au** Gold | 80 201 **Hg** Mercury | 81 204 **Tl** Thallium | 82 207 **Pb** Lead | 83 209 **Bi** Bismuth | 84 209 **Po** Polonium | 85 210 **At** Astatine |

| | | 108 265 **Hs** Hassium | 109 266 **Mt** Meitnerium | 110 269 **Uun** Ununilium | 111 272 **Uuu** Unununium | 112 277 **Uub** Ununbium | | 114 289 **Uuq** Ununquadium | | 116 289 **Uuh** Ununhexium | |

| Sm | 63 152 **Eu** Europium | 64 157 **Gd** Gadolinium | 65 159 **Tb** Terbium | 66 162 **Dy** Dysprosium | 67 165 **Ho** Holmium | 68 167 **Er** Erbium | 69 169 **Tm** Thulium | 70 173 **Yb** Ytterbium | 71 175 **Lu** Lutetium |

| | 95 243 **Am** Americium | 96 247 **Cm** Curium | 97 247 **Bk** Berkelium | 98 251 **Cf** Californium | 99 252 **Es** Einsteinium | 100 257 **Fm** Fermium | 101 258 **Md** Mendelevium | 102 259 **No** Nobelium | 103 262 **Lr** Lawrencium |

The periodic table is broken down into groups and periods. Each element in a group has similar properties. These properties allow one to better understand the relationship between the elements. The staircase line divides metals from nonmetals. Metalloids, such as boron (B) and silicon (Si), are located to the immediate right of the staircase line.

are arranged within periods depending on the number of electron shells that surround the nucleus of their atoms. The outermost electrons determine how elements behave and react with one another. Iron is in period 4 because it has four shells of electrons surrounding its nucleus.

As you read down the chart from top to bottom, the vertical line of elements you see is called a group, or family. Just as you might have similar characteristics to the other members of your family, the elements in a given group have similar characteristics called properties. Iron is in group VIIIB, located near the middle of the periodic table. Overall, the elements found in group VIIIB have the properties typical of metals, such as malleability and the ability to conduct electricity. However, within this group, horizontal similarities are greater than

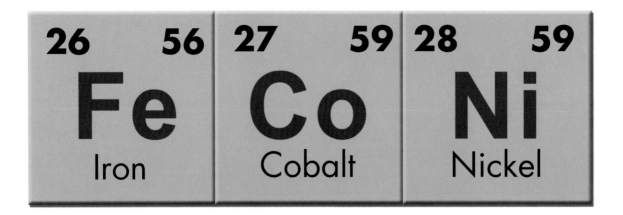

Some elements, known as the transition metals, are also grouped in triads, or groups of three. Iron's triad includes cobalt and nickel. The elements in a triad possess similar chemical properties. The middle element of each triad has a mean, or average, atomic number of the other two elements. The two other transition metal triads are ruthenium (Ru), rhodium (Rh), and palladium (Pd); and osmium (Os), iridium (Ir), and platinum (Pt).

vertical ones. Therefore, each horizontal set of elements is thought of as a triad. Iron, cobalt, and nickel have similar properties, so they have been grouped together to form the iron triad.

All Elements Are Unique

What makes iron different from other elements like oxygen (O) and silver (Ag)? The difference is the number of protons found in the nucleus of the atoms. Since it is the number of protons that makes each element unique, the elements on the periodic table are organized by these numbers. The number of protons that are found in an atom of an element is called the atomic number. On the periodic table, this number is found above and left of the element's symbol. Since iron has twenty-six protons, its atomic number is 26. The fact that iron has twenty-six protons in its nucleus is what makes it iron. If you were able to add one proton to iron's nucleus—which is physically impossible to do—you would have an entirely different element. By adding another proton, you would have an atom of the element cobalt, which has twenty-seven protons. If you were able to take away one of iron's protons, you would have manganese (Mn), which has twenty-five protons in its nucleus.

Atomic Weight

The number that is found in the upper-right corner above an element's symbol on the periodic table is called the atomic weight. Iron has an atomic weight of 55.845. When we know the atomic weight of an element, it helps us to figure out how many neutrons there are in an atom of that element. The atomic weight is the approximate sum of the number of protons and neutrons in the atom. Therefore, knowing that the atomic weight of iron is 55.845 and the atomic number (number of protons) is 26, we can figure out how many neutrons there are in an atom of iron by subtracting the atomic number from the atomic weight:

$$55.845 - 26 = 29.845$$

Iron has approximately thirty neutrons in its nucleus. We can find out a lot of information about iron just by looking at the periodic table!

Uut and Uup Get on the Table

In January 2004, a team of American and Russian scientists announced the creation of two new superheavy elements. Both elements will fill in gaps at the lower end of the periodic table. Element 113 is named ununtrium (Uut); element 115 is named ununpentium (Uup). The new elements are called superheavies because of their enormous atomic weights. However, Uut and Uup will not be given a permanent place on the table until other laboratories have confirmed the existence of the two new elements.

Iron and the Transition Metals

Iron and the other group VIIIB elements are more generally classified as transition metals. The transition metals are located in the middle of the periodic table, from group IIIB on the left to group IIB on the right. Transition metals are unique because many of them are able to do something that other elements cannot: they are able to form more than one positive ion. An ion is a charged particle. It is formed when an atom gains or loses electrons from the shells that surround the nucleus. Atoms are usually electrically neutral, which means they carry no charge. They carry no charge because

Ti	V	Cr	Mn	Fe	Co	Ni	Cu	Zn
Zr	Nb	Mo	Tc	Ru	Rh	Pd	Ag	Cd
Hf	Ta	W	Re	Os	Ir	Pt	Au	Hg
Rf	Db	Sg	Bh	Hs	Mt	Uun	Uuu	Uub

Iron is located in group VIIIB with other transition metals. Many of these metals have similar properties, or characteristics. They are malleable, meaning they can be hammered into different shapes. They are also ductile, meaning they can be pulled to make wire. Transition metals also conduct heat.

they have an equal number of positively charged protons and negatively charged electrons. Basically, the charges cancel out each other. However, if an atom picks up extra negatively charged electrons, it becomes a negatively charged ion (called an anion). In the same manner, if an atom loses electrons, it becomes a

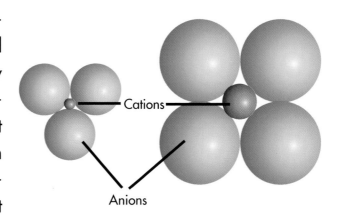

Cations

Anions

Above, negatively charged anions cluster around positively charged cations. An ionic bond results from the attraction between ions with opposite charges. The cluster of ions will form larger building blocks than individual atoms.

positively charged ion (called a cation). Most elements form only one ion by losing or gaining a certain number of electrons. This is not true of the transition metals. Iron, for example, has the ability to form two different ions, Fe^{2+} and Fe^{3+}. Fe^{2+} results when an iron atom loses two electrons, and Fe^{3+} is formed when an iron atom loses three electrons. Iron's ability to lose different numbers of electrons will be of importance when we discuss iron compounds in chapter four.

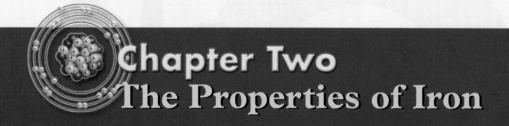

Chapter Two
The Properties of Iron

All elements have characteristic physical and chemical properties. These properties help scientists identify and classify the element. The physical properties of an element are what can be observed without changing the element's identity. Some examples of physical properties are an element's phase at room temperature (whether it's a solid, liquid, or gas), hardness, melting point, and color. The chemical properties of an element describe the element's ability to undergo a chemical change. A chemical change converts one kind of matter into a new kind of matter. An example of a chemical property is iron's ability to react with oxygen to form rust. The chemical properties of an element cannot be observed without changing the identity of the element. For example, in the process of observing how iron rusts, iron is changed from a shiny metal to a crumbly, reddish brown material.

Iron's Phase at Room Temperature

At room temperature, an element is found in one of three phases: solid, liquid, or gas. Knowing the phase, or physical state, of an element at room temperature helps scientists to identify it. Iron is found in the solid phase at room temperature. A solid has a fixed shape and volume. Solids also resist being compressed or having their shape changed.

Iron's Density

Iron's density is 7.86 g/cm^3. Density measures how compact an object is—that is, how much mass it contains per unit volume. Solids are generally denser than liquids, which are, in turn, denser than gases. If you sprinkle iron shavings on water, they will sink. This is because iron is denser than water.

Iron's Hardness

When iron is in its pure form, not mixed with anything else, it is a relatively soft metal. In Mohs' scale, iron has a hardness of 4. For comparison, your fingernail has a hardness of 2.5 and a penny has a hardness of 3.5. Iron is harder than both of these and could scratch them. However, there are a lot of materials that are able to scratch pure iron. In order to make iron harder, other elements are added to it. This is how steel is made.

Elemental properties allow scientists to classify and group the elements. One property is density, which is how compact an object is. This photo demonstrates that iron has greater density than water. The iron filings pass through the water and gather on the bottom of the glass.

Mohs' Scale

Mohs' scale is used to classify the hardness of minerals, metals, and other products. This scale was published in 1822 by Friedrich Mohs, a German mineralogist. He got the idea for the scale from miners, who routinely performed scratch tests. The scale shows ten groups of substances, in order of increasing hardness. Each successive substance is able to scratch the preceding ones and can be scratched by all that follow it. For example, iron is able to scratch copper, but it can be scratched by hardened steel.

Hardness Rating Examples

1	Talc
2	Gypsum, rock salt, fingernail
3	Calcite, copper (Cu)
4	Fluorite, iron
5	Apatite, cobalt (Co)
6	Orthoclase, rhodium (Rh), silicon (Si), tungsten (W)
7	Quartz
8	Topaz, chromium (Cr), hardened steel
9	Corundum, sapphire
10	Diamond

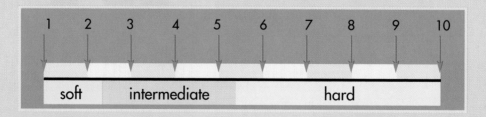

Iron: Conductor of Electricity and Heat

Like all metals, iron conducts electricity and heat. This means that heat and electrical current are able to move through iron. Metals are able to conduct electricity because the electrons from the outer shells of their atoms (valence electrons) are able to move about in what is called a "sea" of electrons. This movement of electrons is an electric charge, or electricity. The sea of electrons that metals have also makes them good conductors of heat. When metals such as iron are heated, the electrons gain more energy. This makes them move about more quickly, distributing the heat throughout the whole metal.

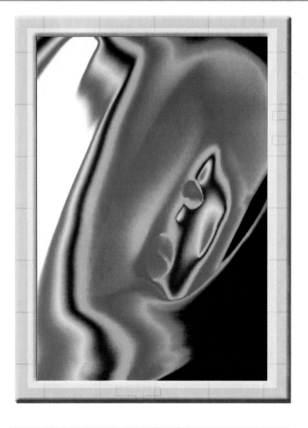

Like all other metals, iron conducts heat, or energy. This infrared picture shows iron conducting heat. The white and red areas indicate extreme heat. Blue and black indicate cooler areas. Several other metals, such as copper, are better conductors and are therefore preferred for industry use.

It takes a lot of heat to pull apart iron atoms. Iron's melting point is 2,795°F (1,535°C, 1,808 K). Because solid iron can handle a lot of heat without melting, it is often used to build things that are exposed to intense heat, such as a car engine.

Once iron is melted into a liquid, the temperature must reach a steamy 4,982°F (2,750°C, 3,023 K) before iron will boil and become a gas. To give you an idea of how hot that is, you can compare this temperature to the temperature found on the surface of the Sun, 9,932°F (5,500°C, 5,773 K). Iron would definitely boil there!

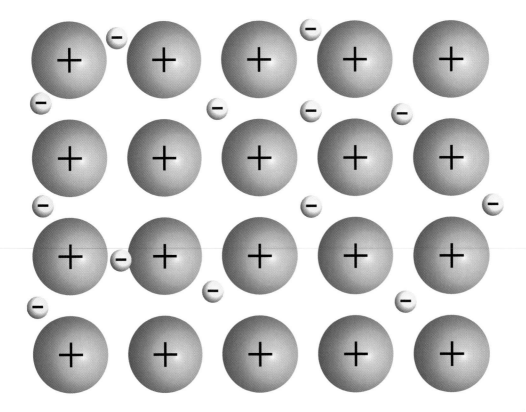

Magnetism is an important property of iron. In their pure form, solid metals are held together by magnetic attraction of their subatomic particles to form a metallic bond *(above)*. This bond results from the metal's positive nuclei and the negative electrons. Each metal atom donates negatively charged electrons that bond with the positively charged nuclei, thus holding the atoms together.

The Magnet Element

One of iron's most important properties is its strong attraction to magnets. Other metals, such as nickel and cobalt, are also magnetic, but iron is much more common than these elements. In fact, if you want to know if an object contains iron, you might test it with a magnet. Magnetism is a force that either pulls things together or forces them apart.

The word "magnetism" comes from the ancient Greek city of Magnesia, a place where lodestones were found in ancient times.

Lodestones are rocks that contain iron and were the first known magnets. Although these rocks had become permanently magnetized, most iron is not permanently magnetic. The fact that iron can become magnetic is due to the structure of the iron atom. The electrons that orbit the nucleus of the iron atom make each atom act like a tiny magnet. If the electrons are lined up in just the right way, a piece of iron becomes magnetized. Iron is made magnetic when it is properly exposed to a magnetic field. A magnetic field can be produced by another magnet or by an electric current. Heating or melting the iron, however, can make the metal lose its magnetism.

You can think of Earth as a huge magnet. Earth's core is made mostly of iron. The core is so hot that the outer part of the core is always

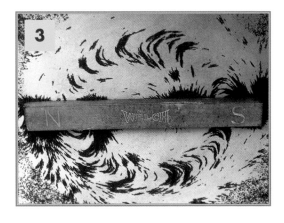

A bar magnet is magnetized into north and south poles. As the magnet is moved, an electric charge is produced *(photo 1)*. This charge causes the iron filings to become magnetized *(photo 2)*. The magnetized iron filings contain a north and a south pole, similar to the bar magnet. The iron filings are then attracted to each other and begin to cluster *(photo 3)*.

liquid. Scientists think that, as Earth spins, the liquid iron swirls around. This movement creates Earth's magnetism.

Earth has magnetic poles, just like a bar magnet. Earth's magnetism is the strongest at these poles. If a small magnet is allowed to turn freely, it will point toward Earth's poles. That is why you are able to use a compass—the magnet inside points toward the North Pole and you are able to find your direction.

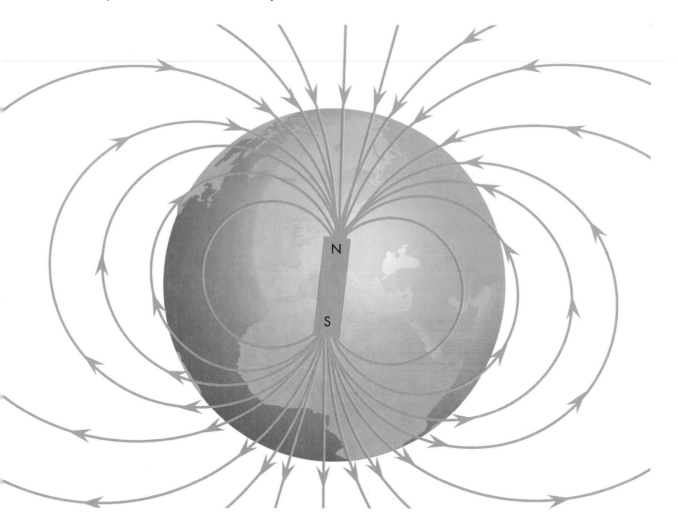

Earth's magnetic field is created by a molten, or liquid, iron-nickel mixture located in Earth's core. This magnetic field helps deflect harmful charged particles released by the Sun. The magnetic field works much like a bar magnet. The lines show the direction of magnetic forces swirling around the field that deflect the charged particles.

What Does Iron Look Like?

Iron, in its pure form, is a somewhat shiny, silvery white metal. However, iron is rarely found in its pure state in nature. This is because, chemically, iron is a fairly reactive metal. This means that it combines with other elements very easily. Iron atoms easily lose two or three of their electrons when they are exposed to other elements like oxygen. When an iron atom loses two or three electrons to some other element, it stops being shiny and takes on a black, green, yellowish orange, or bright red color. This is a chemical change because the identity of iron has changed, such as when rust occurs. Here, the iron atoms have bonded with oxygen atoms and water molecules to turn iron into rust.

Magnetized iron can also make other magnets. Here, iron filings cluster on the ends of a horseshoe magnet. Iron is ferromagnetic, meaning that these iron filings, when brought together will become magnets themselves. Just like a magnet, each iron filing will have north and south poles looking to attach themselves to an opposite charge.

Chapter Three
Where Can Iron Be Found?

Iron is believed to be the most common metal in the universe. As a gas, it is found in the Sun and in many other stars. In fact, Earth's core is made mostly of iron. Iron is also the fourth most common element and the second most abundant metal in Earth's crust. Although iron makes up about 5 percent of Earth's crust, hardly any of it is in its pure form. The only pure iron that is found on Earth's surface arrives from outer space in the form of meteorites. However, a lot of iron can be found combined with other elements.

Iron Ores

Iron ores are rocks that contain iron and other elements. Iron was concentrated in these rocks by natural forces during the formation of Earth's crust millions of years ago. People have been trying to extract iron from these rocks for thousands of years, and it is from these ores that we get the iron we use today. Unlike in ancient times, our ability to get iron from ore has made iron a very commonly used metal. Because iron is so common, it is one of the world's cheapest but most useful metals.

The main ores from which we get iron are hematite, magnetite, and pyrite. These iron ores are mined. Of these iron ores, hematite and magnetite are the richest in iron, containing about 70 percent of the metal by weight. These ores contain iron and oxygen and are called iron oxides. Hematite may be black, brownish red, or dark red. Magnetite is black and has magnetic properties. Pyrite is about half iron and half sulfur (S). You may have heard of pyrite, which is commonly called fool's gold. Its shiny gold-colored appearance fooled many people into thinking that they had found gold! Iron is also extracted from limonite, siderite, and taconite ores.

Types of Iron

There are many different types of iron, but all of these can be grouped into three types: cast iron, wrought iron, and pig iron. Cast iron is an iron alloy and contains iron and two other elements, carbon and silicon (Si). Because it contains carbon, cast iron is very hard. However, cast iron is also very brittle, which means it breaks apart easily. It cannot be shaped

Nations such as Russia, China, Brazil, Australia, and the United States mine nearly 70 percent of the world's iron ore. This iron ore is then turned into one of three main types of iron. Cast iron *(above left)* is often used for cookware. Pig iron is an alloy and is often used to make steel *(above right)*. Wrought iron *(bottom left)* is very malleable and is often used to make fences.

with a hammer even if it is heated to a very high temperature; it will simply break apart. Cast iron is made into useful things when it is melted and then allowed to cool in a mold. The liquid iron takes the shape of the mold, and when it cools and hardens, it keeps that shape. You have seen cast iron in manhole covers, automobile parts, and cookware.

Wrought iron is nearly pure iron. It is mixed with just a tiny bit of a glasslike material called iron silicate. Wrought iron resists corrosion, or rusting, better than cast iron does. Unlike cast iron, wrought iron is malleable. This means that it can be hammered into different shapes. Because it is malleable, wrought iron is used to make metal fences that have a lot of fancy designs. You have also seen wrought iron in coatracks and in the handrails on staircases.

Pig iron is made in a blast furnace. It contains some carbon and a small amount of other elements. At one time, people took the liquid pig iron from the blast furnace and poured it into molds. Pig iron got its name because the molds that it was poured into looked like a group of baby pigs gathered around a mother pig. Today, most pig iron is used to make steel.

Creating Steel

Although some elemental iron is made into iron products, most of it is used to make steel. You can think of steel as refined, or purified, iron. Unlike pure iron, steel is not an element. Steel is produced by refining iron and then mixing it with other elements. Steelmaking involves first removing unwanted substances, such as excess carbon, silicon, or sulfur. To do this, the iron is mixed with limestone and heated to a very high temperature. This is normally done in one of three furnaces: the open hearth, the electric, or the basic oxygen. Once this is done, desired materials are carefully added. These added materials make steel a lot stronger than iron.

Types of Steel

There are thousands of kinds of steel, but these can be grouped into four types: carbon steel, alloy steel, stainless steel, and tool steel. Carbon steel is used more often than any other kind of steel. The properties of this steel depend on how much carbon it contains. The higher the percentage of carbon, the harder the steel is. Carbon steel is made into many products, such as structural beams in buildings, automobile bodies, kitchen appliances, and cans.

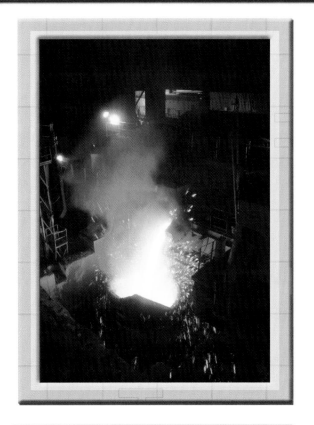

The invention of steel helped change the world in the 1800s. Steel alloys became new and inexpensive metals that were durable, yet could be shaped. Steel would be used to make everything from trains to cars to skyscrapers.

Alloy steel contains some carbon, but its properties depend on the other elements it contains. Each element that is added to alloy steel improves one or more of its properties. Nickel, for example, makes the steel stronger. When manganese is added, it makes the steel harder, tougher, and more resistant to wear. Molybdenum (Mo), another element, increases the steel's hardness and resistance to corrosion. Other elements used in alloy steel include chromium, aluminum (Al), tungsten, copper, titanium, silicon, and vanadium (V).

Stainless steel contains a large amount of the element chromium. Many stainless steels also contain nickel. This type of steel resists corrosion better than any other steel. It is used to make kitchen items such as knives, flatware, pots, and pans. You can also find stainless steel in things such as automobile parts, hospital equipment, and razor blades.

Tool steel is a very hard steel. It is made by a process called tempering. In this process, certain types of carbon steel and alloy steel are heated to a high temperature and then cooled very quickly. Because it is so hard, tool steel is used in metalworking tools such as files, drills, and chisels. Tools made from tool steel are then used to cut other softer metals.

Iron in Your Body

Not only is iron important in bridges, skyscrapers, and automobiles, but it is also important in your body. Iron is part of hemoglobin, which is in your red blood cells. Hemoglobin is responsible for carrying oxygen from your lungs to all the parts of your body. Each hemoglobin molecule contains four iron atoms. Blood and rust are both red for the same reason—because of iron's strong attraction to oxygen. When you breathe, oxygen from the air enters your lungs. Here, it is attracted to the iron in hemoglobin and combines with it to form

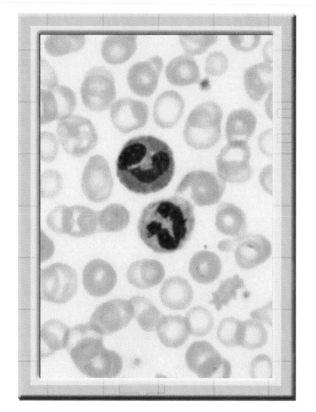

You can't live without iron—literally! Iron plays an important role in your circulatory system. Red blood cells, pictured here, contain iron. The iron helps attract oxygen molecules. The red blood cells then distribute the oxygen throughout your body.

How Much Iron Is in Your Body?

Here is a formula that you can use to calculate how much iron you have in your body. Just multiply your weight by the numbers given.

Your weight in pounds x 0.02724 = the number of grams of iron in your body

Your weight in kilograms x 0.06 = the number of grams of iron in your body

from Websters.com

oxyhemoglobin, the specific hemoglobin that contains oxygen. The oxyhemoglobin is then transported throughout your body by the red blood cells, and oxygen is released wherever it is needed. As you can see, iron is a very important part of your body!

A lack of iron in the body is known as iron deficiency. Someone who does not have enough iron will usually be very tired and not have much energy. Iron deficiency can be due to a diet that is lacking in iron or to an insufficient number of red blood cells. If a person does not have enough red blood cells, he or she is said to be anemic.

Chapter Four
Iron Compounds

Elements chemically combine to form compounds. An important property of metals is their ability to combine chemically with nonmetals to form what are called ionic compounds. Forming an ionic compound between a metallic element and a nonmetallic element involves the transfer of electrons from the metal to the nonmetal. As you already know, iron is able to lose two or three of its electrons. This is important because it means that iron can form more than one compound with a given element. When the ion Fe^{2+} (iron that has lost two electrons) combines with another element, the compound it forms is called a ferrous compound. When Fe^{3+} (iron that has lost three electrons) combines with another element, the compound it forms is called a ferric compound. This can be seen by the way that iron reacts with chlorine, forming two different compounds. When iron loses two electrons to chlorine, it forms ferrous chloride ($FeCl_2$). When iron loses three electrons to chlorine, it forms ferric chloride ($FeCl_3$). Probably the most well-known, and least desirable, chemical reaction of iron is its reaction with water and oxygen to form a ferric compound called rust.

Rust

We have probably all had experience with rust. If you have ever left your bicycle outside in the rain, you have experienced it firsthand!

Rust gathers here on water pipes as a reddish brown substance. The oxidation of iron will cause rust, also known as ferric oxide. Rust is very common with iron materials. Many new technologies have been invented to keep iron products from rusting.

The reddish brown or reddish yellow powder that you found on your bicycle when you finally brought it inside is rust. Rusting requires a metal, oxygen, and water. Iron will not rust in pure water that is free of extra oxygen, and it will not rust in pure oxygen that is moisture free.

When iron, oxygen, and water meet, rust is readily formed. Rust is the common name for ferric oxide and has the chemical formula Fe_2O_3. This is a ferric compound because iron loses three electrons to form it. It is because iron combines so readily with oxygen that we rarely see pure iron in nature.

People do many things in order to keep their iron and steel possessions from rusting. One way to protect these metals is to paint them. The

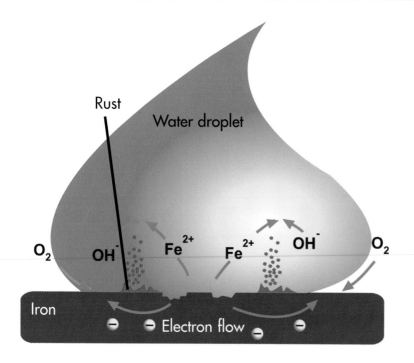

Iron will rust in the presence of oxygen and water. When a water droplet reaches the surface of iron, the metal begins to oxidize. This reaction begins when iron's electrons meet the surface of the water droplet. The electrons move through the metallic iron. This process breaks down the surface of the iron, producing the yellow or brown substance known as rust.

paint on cars forms a barrier between the iron that the car is made of and the water and oxygen in the air. Likewise, many household items have plastic coatings to protect them. A lot of storage shelves are actually wrought iron covered with plastic. Another way to protect iron and steel is to plate, or cover, it with a metal that does not rust, such as chromium (Cr). Car bumpers are sometimes made of chrome-plated steel.

Why Is Mars Red?

Earth is not the only planet that contains iron. Other planets do too. Mars is red because of the iron in its soil. As you know, it takes water and oxygen for iron to rust. Scientists believe that long ago Mars had these substances in its atmosphere. The iron on the surface of the planet reacted with water and formed rust. Rust is everywhere on the planet, which is why Mars is nicknamed the Red Planet.

Because rust is the product of a chemical change, it cannot be separated back into iron and oxygen by any physical means, such as boiling or freezing. Recovering the iron and the oxygen from rust would require another chemical reaction. One way to get rid of rust is by "pickling" the iron. In this process, the rust reacts with an acid. This turns the rust into a harmless substance that can be washed away from the metal. Sometimes hydrochloric acid (HCl) is used for this. This acid reacts with the rust to form a useful iron compound called ferric chloride ($FeCl_3$).

Ferric Chloride

Ferric chloride is a dark-colored crystal. This compound is used mainly for water treatment. It helps to remove impurities from water by causing them to lump together. Once the unwanted material has formed a mass, it can then be filtered out of the water.

Ferric chloride helps to remove soil and other unwanted substances from our drinking water. It is also used by the food, paper, photography, and pharmaceutical industries. All of these industries need to use very

This molecular model demonstrates the crystalline structure of ferric chloride. This iron compound is mainly used in water treatment. When added to untreated water, ferric chloride gathers impurities into a foamy mass on the surface of the water.

pure water. Ferric chloride is also helpful for the environment. Before waste is released into our rivers or lakes, it is treated with ferric chloride. This makes the waste safe enough so that it will not harm the organisms that live in the water.

Ferric chloride is also sometimes used as a disinfectant to destroy harmful bacteria, viruses, and other disease-causing materials. These things are not only harmful to us, but they also give water a bad taste, an odor, and a funny color. Ferric chloride treatment helps to make drinking water look and taste better, and it also helps sewage smell better!

Ferrous Chloride

Ferrous chloride ($FeCl_2$) is formed when hot chlorine gas is passed over iron. This is a ferrous compound because iron has donated two electrons to the chlorine. Ferrous chloride is a colorless, crystalline substance. Like ferric chloride, it is used for sewage treatment. However, ferrous chloride is also used for dyeing fabric.

Ferrous chloride is what is known as a mordant. Mordants keep the color from fading from fabric. When dyeing something with a natural dye, which is obtained from plants or animals, it is necessary to use a mordant. If a mordant isn't used, the color will fade when the fabric is exposed to sunlight or is washed. Ferrous chloride binds these natural dyes to the fabric, holding them there tightly so that they cannot be washed out.

Ferrous Sulfate

Ferrous sulfate ($FeSO_4$) is a green crystalline substance. Like ferrous chloride, ferrous sulfate is used as a mordant. It is also used in water purification. However, ferrous sulfate also performs a much more important task. This iron compound is used to treat iron-deficiency anemia. Some people are at a higher risk of developing this anemia than

Heated iron reacts violently with gaseous chlorine. Here, steel wool (which contains iron) is heated and dipped into a container of chlorine gas *(photo 1)*. The iron reacts violently with the chlorine to produce ferric chloride *(photo 2)*. After several moments, the ferric chloride begins to settle, creating a thick, rust-colored gas *(photo 3)*.

other people. High-risk groups include pregnant women, infants, children, and adolescents. These people need extra iron because they are growing. People whose diets are low in iron or whose bodies have trouble absorbing iron are also at risk.

Without enough iron, red blood cells don't mature properly. They stay small and pale and are unable to properly carry oxygen. That is why an anemic person does not have the energy to complete simple tasks. To remedy this condition, a doctor may prescribe ferrous sulfate in pill form to provide the iron that the body needs in order to make red blood cells.

Chapter Five
Iron and You

As you read earlier, iron is an important part of your body. That's why it is important that you provide iron for your body to use. You can do this by eating foods that are high in iron. The best source of iron for your body is red meat. It not only contains a lot of iron, but the iron is easily absorbed, or taken in, by your body. Some other foods, such as beans and lentils, also contain a lot of iron. However, the iron from these foods is a lot harder for your body to absorb. Some foods, like fruits and vegetables, contain vitamin C, which helps your body absorb the iron from the other foods you eat.

Some foods do not naturally contain a lot of iron, but have iron added to them. These are iron-fortified foods. Many breakfast cereals have iron added to them. Iron filings are often added to cereals, but don't worry, it is good for you!

Eating Iron

According to the Institute of Food Research, people need different amounts of iron in their diets, depending upon how old they are. Toddlers (ages one to three years old) need at least 3.7 milligrams of iron per day. Young children (ages four to six years) require at least 3.3 mg every day. Older children (ages seven to ten years) should eat at least

Iron in Your Cereal

You can separate tiny pieces of iron from your cereal with just a few materials. You will need a plastic bag that you can seal, warm water, a large magnet, and iron-fortified cereal (make sure that the label on the cereal says "reduced iron" or "100% iron").

First you will have to crush the flakes of cereal into tiny pieces the size of a pinhead. Mix this cereal in your plastic bag with enough warm water to make it very soupy. After you seal your bag, press your magnet to the outside of the bag. The iron filings will actually collect on the inside of the bag near the magnet! The iron will look like small dark dots. If you have any trouble seeing the iron, try using a magnifying glass.

4.7 mg of iron a day. Teenagers (ages eleven to eighteen) need more iron than any other age group. Teenage girls require at least 8.0 mg of iron, while teenage boys need 6.1 mg.

This chart shows approximately how much iron some common foods provide.

Food	Serving size (grams)	Amount of iron (mg)
Grilled steak (1 medium)	144	4.3
Fried liver (1 slice)	40	3
Prunes (6)	100	1.8
Lima beans	75	1.8
Cooked chicken or turkey	90	1.6
Green vegetables	75	1.5
Cereal (with iron added)	30	1.3
Egg (1)	50	1.1
Whole wheat bread (1 slice)	36	1.0
White bread (1 slice)	36	0.6

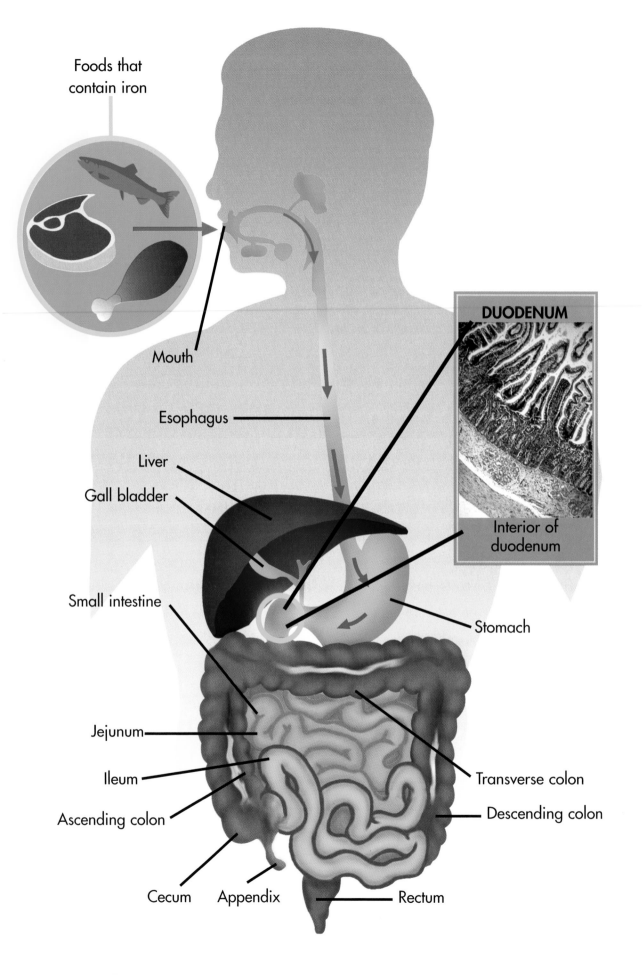

Foods that contain iron

Mouth

Esophagus

Liver

Gall bladder

Small intestine

Jejunum

Ileum

Ascending colon

Cecum

Appendix

Rectum

DUODENUM

Interior of duodenum

Stomach

Transverse colon

Descending colon

Iron is essential for the human body to work properly. Foods such as fish, red meat, and chicken are high in iron. When food is ingested *(opposite)*, acids in the stomach turn iron into ferric iron. This is then absorbed by the duodenum in the small intestine *(inset, opposite)*. It then enters the bloodstream and eventually the bone marrow *(right)*. The bone marrow produces red blood cells, which transport oxygen throughout the body.

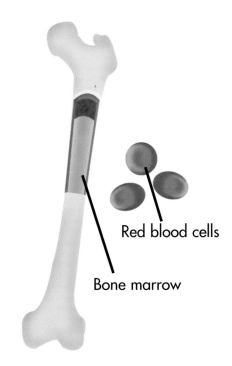

Red blood cells

Bone marrow

Magnetic Money

We know that magnets are attracted to iron, steel, and some other metals, but are they attracted to money? Find a magnet and gather some money together to see.

In the United States, the metal that has been used to make pennies has changed over time. Currently, pennies are made of copper and zinc (Zn). Neither of these metals are magnetic, so pennies would not be attracted to the magnet. However, in 1943, pennies were made of steel, so these pennies would be attracted to the magnet. If you find one of these pennies, hold on to it. It is a collector's item!

You will find that none of the other U.S. coins are attracted to magnets, not even nickels. Even though nickel is a magnetic metal, just like iron, nickel coins do not contain enough of the metal to make them magnetic.

Surprisingly, dollar bills are attracted to magnets! No, paper is not magnetic, but the ink on the paper contains iron. Why is the ink made like that? Well, did you ever wonder how the bill-changing machines know

Iron can even be found in places where you might not expect it. Paper currency has small amounts of iron. This comes in handy at bank machines, which dispense money. The machines use magnets to grab the money.

how much change to give you? It is the magnetic ink. The machines can tell the difference between the bills ($1, $5, $10, etc.) by the pattern of the ink on them. This also keeps people from making fake bills with a photocopy machine. If a bill does not have the magnetic ink, the machine will recognize it as counterfeit.

The Compass

A compass is a device that you can use to help you find your way. At the center of a compass is a needle made out of magnetized iron. No matter where you are, the needle on a compass always points north, toward the magnetic North Pole. Although we now have more complex methods of finding our way, such as maps and GPS (global positioning system), people have always relied on compasses to get around.

Iron Is Everywhere!

Test everyday items around you to see if they are made of iron. Find some metallic items like staples, coins, nails, paper clips, jewelry, and soda cans. Which ones do you think are magnetic? Get a magnet and see! The objects that are attracted to the magnet are probably made of iron. Even

Make Your Own Compass

You can make a compass that is very similar to the ones people made hundreds of years ago. Here are the things you will need to make a compass:
- A large needle
- Something that floats (such as a cork or a plastic cap from a milk jug)
- A bowl of water
- A magnet (you can probably find one on your refrigerator or on your can opener)

   First, you will have to magnetize the needle. Stroke the needle with the magnet. The direction should be from the back of the needle to the point. This will make the needle magnetic. Place your float in the middle of the bowl of water and lay the magnetic needle on top. The needle and float will slowly turn so that pointed end of the needle points north. Now you have your very own compass! Try turning the needle around and see what happens.

though other metals are also magnetic, iron is used much more often. Take your magnet with you the next time you go out. Try sticking your magnet to different objects. Which ones do you think are made of iron?

   Each element on the periodic table plays its role perfectly to create everything in our universe. Like all the other elements in the periodic table, iron is essential to life on Earth. Every day, every minute, every second, you are surrounded by iron. It is found in outer space and right here on Earth, both on the surface and deep within Earth's core. As you have seen, iron from the surface of Earth is used to make steel—one of the greatest inventions and most useful materials ever created. Iron is in the food you eat, and it is even found in you!

The Periodic Table of Elements

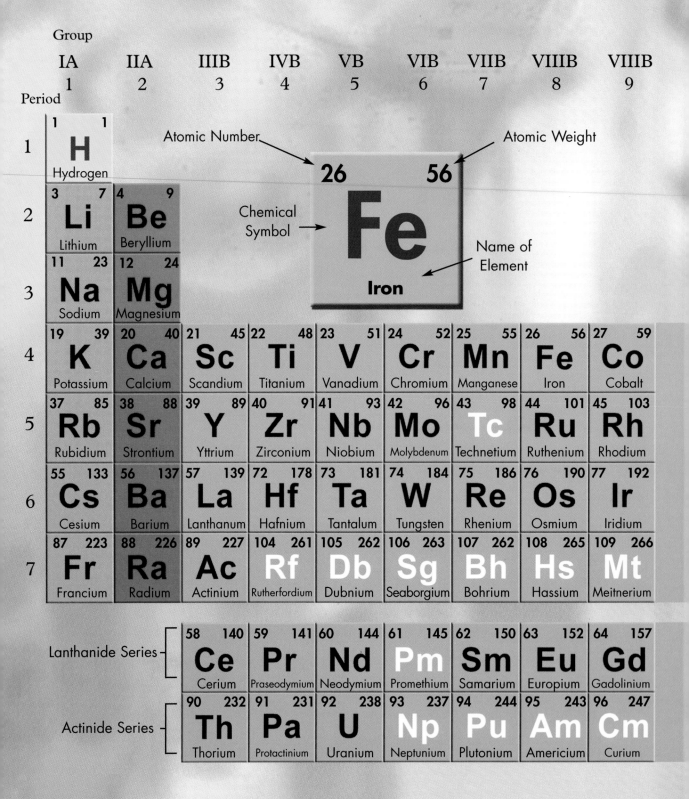

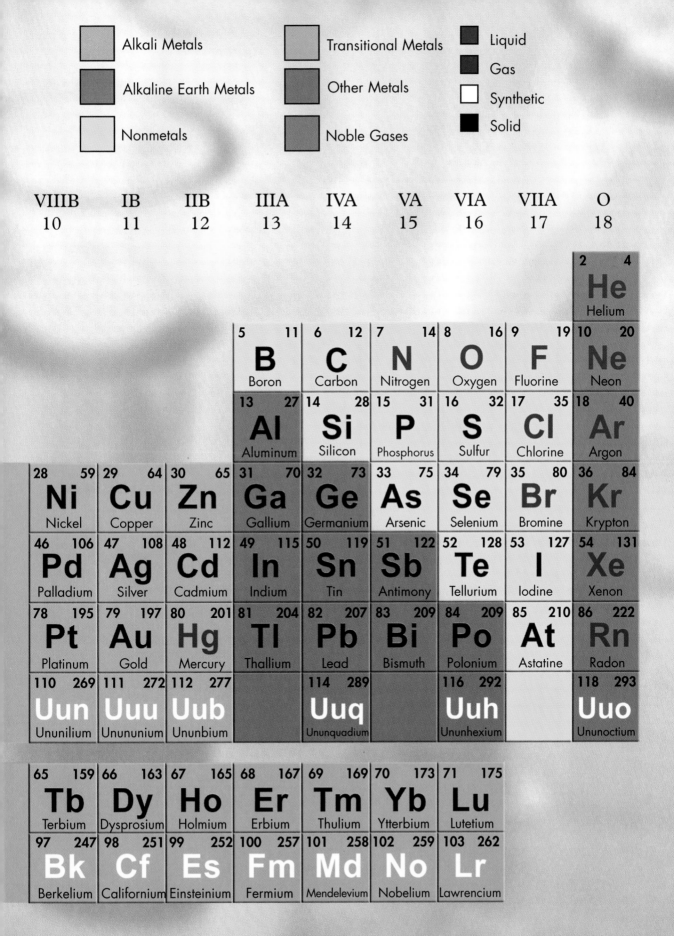

Alkali Metals
Alkaline Earth Metals
Nonmetals
Transitional Metals
Other Metals
Noble Gases
Liquid
Gas
Synthetic
Solid

VIIIB	IB	IIB	IIIA	IVA	VA	VIA	VIIA	O
10	11	12	13	14	15	16	17	18

								2 · 4 **He** Helium
			5 · 11 **B** Boron	6 · 12 **C** Carbon	7 · 14 **N** Nitrogen	8 · 16 **O** Oxygen	9 · 19 **F** Fluorine	10 · 20 **Ne** Neon
			13 · 27 **Al** Aluminum	14 · 28 **Si** Silicon	15 · 31 **P** Phosphorus	16 · 32 **S** Sulfur	17 · 35 **Cl** Chlorine	18 · 40 **Ar** Argon
28 · 59 **Ni** Nickel	29 · 64 **Cu** Copper	30 · 65 **Zn** Zinc	31 · 70 **Ga** Gallium	32 · 73 **Ge** Germanium	33 · 75 **As** Arsenic	34 · 79 **Se** Selenium	35 · 80 **Br** Bromine	36 · 84 **Kr** Krypton
46 · 106 **Pd** Palladium	47 · 108 **Ag** Silver	48 · 112 **Cd** Cadmium	49 · 115 **In** Indium	50 · 119 **Sn** Tin	51 · 122 **Sb** Antimony	52 · 128 **Te** Tellurium	53 · 127 **I** Iodine	54 · 131 **Xe** Xenon
78 · 195 **Pt** Platinum	79 · 197 **Au** Gold	80 · 201 **Hg** Mercury	81 · 204 **Tl** Thallium	82 · 207 **Pb** Lead	83 · 209 **Bi** Bismuth	84 · 209 **Po** Polonium	85 · 210 **At** Astatine	86 · 222 **Rn** Radon
110 · 269 **Uun** Ununilium	111 · 272 **Uuu** Unununium	112 · 277 **Uub** Ununbium		114 · 289 **Uuq** Ununquadium		116 · 292 **Uuh** Ununhexium		118 · 293 **Uuo** Ununoctium

65 · 159 **Tb** Terbium	66 · 163 **Dy** Dysprosium	67 · 165 **Ho** Holmium	68 · 167 **Er** Erbium	69 · 169 **Tm** Thulium	70 · 173 **Yb** Ytterbium	71 · 175 **Lu** Lutetium
97 · 247 **Bk** Berkelium	98 · 251 **Cf** Californium	99 · 252 **Es** Einsteinium	100 · 257 **Fm** Fermium	101 · 258 **Md** Mendelevium	102 · 259 **No** Nobelium	103 · 262 **Lr** Lawrencium

Glossary

alloy A mixture of a metal and one or more other elements, usually metals.

anion An atom that picks up extra electrons and becomes a negatively charged ion.

atom The smallest part of an element.

cation An atom that loses electrons and becomes a positively charged ion.

chemical reaction A change in which one kind of matter is turned into another kind of matter.

crust The surface layer of the earth.

crystalline Composed of crystals, with a regular pattern.

ferric compound A compound of iron and another element or elements in which the iron atom(s) has given up three electrons.

ferrous compound A compound of iron and another element or elements in which the iron atom(s) has given up two electrons.

fortified Having something added to it to make it better.

ion A charged atom.

mass The measure of the amount of matter in something.

matter What things are made of. Matter takes up space and has mass.

pole The part of a magnet where its magnetism is the strongest. There are two poles (north and south) on a magnet.

volume The amount of space that something occupies.

For More Information

The Exploratorium
3601 Lyon Street
San Francisco, CA 94123
Directions: (415) 561-0399
Web site: http://www.exploratorium.edu

Association for Iron & Steel
186 Thorn Hill Road
Warrendale, PA 15086
(724) 776-1535
Web site: http://www.aistech.org

Michigan Iron Industry Museum
73 Forge Road
Negaunee, MI 49866
(906) 475-7857
Web site: http://www.michigan.gov/hal/0,1607,7-160-17447_18595_18611---,00.html

Web Sites

Due to the changing nature of Internet links, the Rosen Publishing Group, Inc., has developed an online list of Web sites related to the subject of this book. This site is updated regularly. Please use this link to access the list:

http://www.rosenlinks.com/uept/iron

For Further Reading

Greenwood, N. N., and A. Earnshaw. *Chemistry of the Elements.* Oxford, England: Pergamon Press, 1984.

Hudson, John. *The History of Chemistry.* New York: Routledge, 1992.

Newton, David E. *The Chemical Elements.* New York: Franklin Watts, 1994.

Verschuur, Gerrit L. *Hidden Attraction: The History and Mystery of Magnetism.* New York: Oxford University Press, 1996.

Bibliography

Ebbing, Darrell D. *General Chemistry.* 4th ed. Boston: Houghton Mifflin Company, 1993.

Heiserman, David L. *Exploring Chemical Elements and Their Compounds.* New York: McGraw-Hill Trade, 1991.

Stwertka, Albert. *A Guide to the Elements.* 2nd ed. New York: Oxford University Press, 2002.

Tocci, Salvatore. *Experiments with Magnets.* New York: Children's Press, 2002.

Weeks, Mary Elvira. *Discovery of the Elements.* Easton, PA: Journal of Chemical Education, 1968.

About the Author

Heather Elizabeth Hasan graduated college summa cum laude with a dual major in biochemistry and chemistry. She currently resides in Montgomery County, Maryland, with her husband, Omar, and her son, Samuel.

Photo Credits

Cover, pp. 1, 7, 9, 11, 12, 14, 15, 18, 20, 22, 32, 33, 38, 39, 42-43 by Tahara Hasan; p. 5 © Ted Kinsman/Photo Researchers, Inc.; pp. 17, 21, 35 by Maura McConnell; p. 19 © Eye of Science/Photo Researchers, Inc.; p. 23 © TekImage/Photo Researchers, Inc.; p. 25 (top left) © Becky Luigart-Stayner/Corbis; p. 25 (top right) © Charles E. Rotkin/Corbis; p. 25 (bottom left) © Gary Conner/Index Stock; p. 27 © Paul Shambroom/Photo Researchers, Inc.; pp. 28, 31, 38 (inset) © 2000-2004 Custom Medical Stock Photo; p. 40 © Royalty-Free/Corbis.

Special thanks to Rosemarie Alken and Westtown School, in Westtown, Pennsylvania.

Designer: Tahara Hasan; **Editor:** Charles Hofer